Supplement to *British Book*

SHERIDAN

By W. A. DARLINGTON

PUBLISHED FOR
THE BRITISH COUNCIL
and the NATIONAL BOOK LEAGUE
by LONGMANS, GREEN & CO.
LONDON. NEW YORK. TORONTO

Revised Price
2s. 6d. net

W. A. Darlington, who has written this appreciation of Sheridan to honour the bi-centenary of the dramatist's birth, is an author, journalist, and playwright of many accomplishments. For the last twenty-five years he has been one of the best-known critics in Great Britain, and he summed up his experience of theatre-going in his widely read autobiography, *I Do What I Like*.

He was born in Taunton in 1890, and after going to school at Shrewsbury won a classical scholarship to St. John's College, Cambridge, where he took honours in classics and English Literature. During the first world war he held a commission in the 7th Northumberland Fusiliers, and began contributing to *Punch*. In 1920 he joined the staff of the *Daily Telegraph* as dramatic critic, and in 1925 was appointed dramatic editor of the paper. He became London Theatre correspondent of the *New York Times* in 1939, and has been President of the Critics Circle, and a lecturer on playwriting at East London College, London University.

W. A. Darlington's books include his humorous best seller, *Alf's Button*, successful also as a stage play, and three times filmed, with its sequels, as well as his serious critical works, *Through the Fourth Wall, Literature in the Theatre*, and *The Actor and his Audience*. He is also the author of biographies of J. M. Barrie and of Sheridan, to whom he here returns with enthusiasm.

Bibliographical Series
of Supplements to ' British Book News '

*

GENERAL EDITOR
T. O. Beachcroft

SHERIDAN
from a pastel by J. RUSSELL, 1788, *in the National Portrait Gallery.*

SHERIDAN

1751—1816

By W. A. DARLINGTON

PUBLISHED FOR
THE BRITISH COUNCIL
and the NATIONAL BOOK LEAGUE
BY LONGMANS, GREEN & CO., LONDON, NEW YORK, TORONTO

LONGMANS, GREEN & CO. LTD.
6 & 7 Clifford Street, London, W.1
Also at Melbourne and Cape Town

LONGMANS, GREEN & CO. INC.
55 Fifth Avenue, New York, 3

LONGMANS, GREEN & CO.
215 Victoria Street, Toronto, 1

ORIENT LONGMANS LTD.
Bombay, Calcutta, Madras

First published in 1951

*Printed in Great Britain by Benham and Company Limited
Colchester*

CONTENTS

SHERIDAN *page* 5
A SELECT BIBLIOGRAPHY 27

¶ RICHARD BRINSLEY SHERIDAN was born in Dublin on 30 October 1751. He died on 7 July 1816, and was buried in Westminster Abbey.

SHERIDAN

WHEN David Garrick's health compelled him to retire from the stage in 1776 he not only relinquished his position as manager of Drury Lane theatre but decided to sell his half-interest in the property, which was then valued at £35,000. Various candidates presented themselves but the one who obtained Garrick's favourable notice was a charming but casual young Irishman barely twenty-five years old who had not even the elementary recommendation of possessing £35,000, or indeed any considerable sum of money at all. Nevertheless Garrick fell in with the involved and ingenious schemes by which young Richard Brinsley Sheridan proposed to obtain the money, and in doing so made it fairly clear that he was in effect handing on the torch to the man whom he thought most likely to be a worthy successor to himself. By this act Garrick was condemning Drury Lane to many years of uncertainty and doubt, for Sheridan had strange views of the way a great institution should be run. Also it is likely that in 1776 Garrick felt more certain of his young successor's devotion to the stage than he might have a few years later in 1780, when Sheridan ceased to be a dramatist in regular practice and became a politician. Nevertheless history has proved that Garrick's choice, unsatisfactory though it must have seemed to many at the time, was the best that he could have made. Except for Garrick himself, Drury Lane has never had a more distinguished manager than this casual young genius, the bi-centenary of whose birth we are celebrating in this year of grace, 1951.

Garrick's precise reasons for his action are easy enough to understand. Sheridan's father was an actor who had at one time held so high a position on the Dublin stage that he conceived himself to be, and in one or two specially suitable parts actually was, worthy to be considered Garrick's rival. Sheridan's mother was not only a friend of Garrick's but had written for him a play, *The Discovery*, in which Garrick had found one of his favourite parts. What is more, in the previous year, 1775, Richard Sheridan had blazed suddenly into fame as a dramatist with two original plays and the libretto for a comic opera, all three of which had been produced with success at Covent Garden theatre. A young man who, with the theatre in his blood, had made such a flying start on his career as a dramatist must surely be destined to be a leader in that profession for very many years to come.

Garrick himself had never wavered in his allegiance to the stage, and doubtless found it impossible to imagine that his young friend would do so either. He must have known that the young man had social as well as theatrical ambitions, for Sheridan had already made this very clear; but Garrick too had had social ambitions, and had been able to gratify them by making himself a place in the great world such as no man of the theatre had ever been allowed to occupy before. It is a safe guess that he regarded Sheridan as a man after his own heart in this matter. If so, he made a cardinal error. Garrick was through and through an artist of the stage and wished to be nothing else. Sheridan was only an artist because he could not help himself, and he had no intention of letting this fact shape his life.

In order to understand Sheridan's career it is necessary always to keep in mind that he had only one deep ambition, and that this had nothing to do specifically either with politics or the theatre. His determination was from the first to be an important figure in the little Great World of London society. In the eighteenth century this was not the ignoble aspiration which it would appear to-day. It is almost true to say that if a man desired to live the perfect life he had in those days to be both well-born and rich. Unless he could fulfil both these conditions he could appear in high society only as a hanger-on. Sheridan seems from the first to have felt himself destined for great things, and to have set himself at a very early age to achieve a position which, on the face of it, seemed utterly out of his reach. He was very well acquainted with the Great World of fashion, for his family had lived successively in Dublin, London, and Bath; and to Bath every year in due season the fashionable world migrated. Sheridan's father had by this time made up his mind to the fact that London no longer regarded him as a leading actor, and had resigned himself—not always with a good grace—to a prosperous but comparatively undistinguished existence as a teacher of elocution. His son Richard had, therefore, opportunities of mixing with great ladies and gentlemen and observing their manners and foibles. This stood him in wonderful stead when he came to write plays about them, but it was not for this purpose that he sought their company. He wanted to be one of them—one of the most important of them.

He had the asset of decent birth. The O'Sheridans had been a family of note in Ireland, and he claimed a vague descent from them. His grandfather had been Doctor Thomas Sheridan, an eccentric divine of considerable fame as a schoolmaster and also known for his long friendship with Dean Swift. But these advantages were made almost valueless by the fact that his father, the second Thomas Sheridan, had gone on the stage. It had been, indeed, a rather curious step for this young man to take. He was of a serious and even pedantic turn of mind. He was educated at Westminster School and Trinity College, Dublin, and was in the middle of what seemed likely to be a very distinguished scholastic career when his cheerfully shiftless father died leaving a young family behind him. It was at this point that the younger Thomas made the strange decision to turn actor. He did so with remarkable success.

In those days, however, actors still ranked socially on much the same level as upper servants, and if Thomas Sheridan had deliberately set out to stand in the way of his younger son Dick's chosen career he could hardly have done so more thoroughly than by his own choice. Thomas valued what he had acquired at Westminster, and so Dick was given the advantage of Harrow; but everybody in the school was inclined to look upon him as 'a player's son', so

that he had only a part of the benefit which ' the education
of a gentleman ' might have given him. Still, his brilliance
of mind and his native charm made him popular in the end
with his schoolfellows, and so he entered upon his life as a
young man about town not very seriously handicapped by
his origin.

Fate played into his hands almost at once by turning him
into a romantic hero. Among the closest friends of the
Sheridan family in Bath were the Linleys, a tribe of musical
geniuses with no pretension to gentility but with almost
every other gift that was needed to bring them fame and
fortune in their own walk of life. Thomas Linley, the
father of the family, was a composer of some reputation,
and most of his children either sang or played with a high
professional degree of skill. Elizabeth Linley, the eldest
daughter, and Thomas Sheridan were colleagues. They
used to give a joint entertainment of which Sheridan's share
now sounds quite incredibly ponderous, being a solemn
discourse, with examples, on the importance of oratory.
To provide jam in which this portentous pill might be
swallowed, Elizabeth sang at intervals during the programme.

Elizabeth Linley is one of those characters whose glamour
continues long after they are dead. Every biographer
except one—and that one a stern Victorian matron—who
has written about Richard Sheridan has fallen in love with
Elizabeth Linley. At sixteen she was famous all over the
country both as a beauty and as a singer, and she was the
toast of Bath. She was modest and had no desire for
notoriety, yet she could not keep out of the public eye. An
elderly landowner named Long fell in love with her and
proposed marriage. Her mother, who had a ferocious
greed for money, browbeat the girl into acquiescence.
Then Long backed out, and had to pay £3,000 as compensation. Foote turned these events into a comedy called *The
Maid of Bath*, and Elizabeth was for a time the chief subject
of Bath gossip.

After this, another lover appeared on the scene—a man called Matthews whose intentions from the first were strictly dishonourable. He persecuted the unhappy girl until she sought the advice of her chief friend, Alicia Sheridan, the elder of Dick's two sisters. Alicia took Dick into her confidence, and between them they concocted a plan by which Elizabeth was to take refuge in France, whither she was to fly with Dick as her escort. The young couple—Dick was twenty-one and Elizabeth seventeen—eloped in a post-chaise to London on 18 March 1772. In the course of this adventure they fell in love with each other, and in Calais they went through some kind of marriage ceremony. Nevertheless when Thomas Linley caught up with them at Lille he found that Dick Sheridan had treated his daughter in accordance with all the highest ideals of chivalry. He brought the girl back to Bath and the 'marriage' was temporarily forgotten. Bath was all agog over the affair, with excitement which did not die down when Dick fought two duels with Matthews and was badly hurt in the second of them. The parents of both lovers opposed the match, but romance was too strong for worldly wisdom. Dick and Elizabeth were married at Marylebone Church on 13 April 1773 with the consent of Thomas Linley, but without that of Thomas Sheridan, who exhibited to his undutiful son that 'damned disinheriting countenance' which Richard later bestowed on Sir Anthony Absolute.

The young couple spent an idyllic honeymoon in a cottage. Then, still in the same cottage at East Burnham, they tried to settle down to a quiet life while Dick, who had now decided to go to the Bar, worked at the law. This was probably the wisest idea he could have had regarding his future, for the Bar was a gentleman's occupation; and considering the great forensic gifts which he was to exhibit later in life, he could hardly have helped becoming a leading advocate and winning great wealth. However, it was not to be. His legal training ended very soon after it had begun.

He was next heard of in a house in Orchard Street far beyond any means that he can possibly have had, entertaining on a large scale. The chief attraction at these 'Orchard Street Concerts', as they were called, was young Mrs. Sheridan's singing. Society flocked to obtain for nothing the treat for which it had hitherto been required to pay Thomas Linley large sums of money (it is reckoned that his elder daughter had brought him in an income of about £1,000 a year). The young Sheridans had no income at all, and it is not known what they were living on unless it may have been some part of the money paid over to Elizabeth from the recalcitrant Mr. Long. It is said that Elizabeth wanted to keep the home going by singing professionally; it is also said that Dick refused, on her behalf, within a few months of their marriage, offers amounting to over £3,000—an immense sum in those days. Dick's detractors, who have never lacked either numbers or venom, put this down to an insensate family pride; but a more charitable interpretation of his conduct, and one which has the advantage of taking into consideration the underlying determination and strength of his character, is to say that he here showed most clearly the realization that if he was to get what he wanted he must not allow either himself or his wife to be classed as a paid performer. He may also be given the credit for not wishing to live on his wife's earnings, for it was at this point that he relaxed his intention to cut away, as far as possible, from his theatrical associations. Acting was not a gentleman's occupation, but writing plays might be. Sometime towards the end of 1774 he told his father-in-law that he had written a comedy which would soon be in rehearsal at Covent Garden, and that he hoped to make £600 by it. Accordingly on 17 January 1775 *The Rivals* was presented to the public.

The result must have been a dreadful shock to Richard Sheridan, for the play was a flat failure and was withdrawn after two nights. This brought in another flood of tempting offers of concert engagements for Elizabeth, and in the

Creevey Papers there is a story, probably no more credible than most of Creevey's, that Elizabeth herself wrote to her husband, 'My dear Dick, I am delighted. I always knew that it was impossible you could make anything by writing plays; so now there is nothing for it but my beginning to sing publicly again, and we shall have as much money as we like.' These words are quite out of character with anything else that she is recorded to have said to him, but if she wrote them she was in for a quick and salutary surprise. Dick Sheridan was not a theatre genius for nothing. Where most young authors would have been crushed and despairing, he remained serene. He went to work again on his manuscript in the light of experience and on 28 January, eleven days after the failure, the play was produced again with instant success and has remained in the theatrical repertory ever since.

Once committed to the theatre Sheridan went straight forward. His next production was a short piece called *St. Patrick's Day; or the Scheming Lieutenant*. He wrote this especially for an Irish actor named Clinch who had given an excellent performance as Sir Lucius O'Trigger in the second production of *The Rivals* (whereas Lee, who had played the part at first, had been so bad as to be a major cause of the play's failure). This play was produced on 2 May 1775 and can hardly have brought its author much money. But later in the same year, on 21 November at the same theatre, he and Linley scored a joint artistic and financial triumph with their comic opera *The Duenna*. This had a run of seventy-five nights, which for those days was quite phenomenal and actually beat by ten performances the run of Gay's *Beggar's Opera*. There could now be no more question of Elizabeth having, or being allowed, to sing in public. Nor could there be any question of Dick Sheridan's acceptance by the Great World. Reigning beauties, such as Georgiana, Duchess of Devonshire and Mrs. Crewe, were now among his intimate friends. The Duchess, who had at first debated seriously whether she could admit a player's son to her acquaintance, was now completely captivated. In the end she became so intimate a friend that we hear of her remaining at Chatsworth two months longer than her intention, in order to enjoy Sheridan's society, while the expenses of a house she had taken at Bath wasted themselves week by week.

In the London of those days a big success at either of the two patent theatres was bound to tell heavily on the fortunes of the other. The run of *The Duenna* notoriously caused much worry to Garrick at Drury Lane, and it was freely, if rather heartlessly, said that 'The old woman would be the death of the old man'. Garrick survived the ordeal, but it may have hastened his determination to retire, and it certainly decided his choice of a successor.

On 24 June 1776 Sheridan signed the agreement which made over Garrick's half of Drury Lane to himself and his two partners, Thomas Linley and Doctor James Ford the court physician. Ford paid £15,000 and Linley £10,000, sums which each could well afford, but exactly how Sheridan's share, also of £10,000, was found is a mystery shrouded in a mass of complicated arithmetic which need not concern us. Garrick was satisfied and it was agreed by all parties that Sheridan was to be the new manager of the theatre. The other half of the property was owned by a young man called Lacy, who seemed content to be a sleeping partner. Soon, however, he showed a desire to divide his share with some friends who looked likely to interfere with the management of the theatre. Sheridan saw that this would make his position difficult and organized a strike of actors, who were as ready as actors always have been to side with an accredited man of the theatre against any mere 'bricks-and-mortar man'. The result was that Lacy abandoned his idea of selling and kept his half of the property until Sheridan himself was able to take it over from him two years later.

In the first months of his management Sheridan

introduced no new plays. He was content for the moment to use what he found in Garrick's repertory. Most of the Restoration comedies, however, had now become too coarse for the increasingly refined public taste, and he restored one of the least likely of these to cause offence, Vanbrugh's *The Relapse*, to its place on the stage by rewriting it under the title, *A Trip to Scarborough*. He produced this in February 1777 ; and its success gave him a breathing space to put the final touches to his own masterpiece, *The School for Scandal*.

One of Sheridan's traits which seemed to irritate not only his more solemn contemporaries but also a great number of people in later ages was the fact that nobody ever saw him at work. One of his early tutors remarked on this to him in the words, ' How it comes to pass that you are ever in appearance indolent without really being so, I cannot conjecture '. No better example of this maddening habit exists than *The School for Scandal*, which obviously must have been the fruit of a great deal of very hard work. There still exist draft copies of parts of it which show that its final form was a fusion of two separate comedies, one dealing with the Teazles and the other with Lady Sneerwell and her crew of scandalmongers. Nevertheless the comedy came as such a surprise to London that a great many people refused to believe that it was Sheridan's work at all. There was an elaborate rumour that the play had been written by a young lady, the daughter of a merchant in Thames Street, who had sent the manuscript to Drury Lane and had then very conveniently died. This story was not only widely believed at the time, but was solemnly printed by Sheridan's earlier biographers. No calumny against this young man whose casual brilliance so infuriated them seemed too silly to be accepted.

He was most characteristically casual in this particular case, for in the end the last scenes of the play had to be written in the theatre and against time. At the end of his script Sheridan scribbled the words, ' Finished, thank God.'

R.B.S.'; under which Hopkins, the Drury Lane prompter, added ' Amen '. The play was staged on 8 May 1777 and it met with such thunders of applause that a passer-by in the street ran for his life thinking that the building was going to collapse. It is, almost by common consent, the finest example of the comedy of manners in the English language and its continued stageworthiness at all times since it was written has been unquestioned. It was a steady standby to Sheridan both as author and as theatre-manager for the rest of his career, for it could always be put into the bill at a moment's notice after a failure, and could be relied upon to restore the theatre's finances.

Doubtless it was the great success of this play which enabled Sheridan to take over Lacy's half of the theatre as early as 1778. Once again the arithmetic was complicated but its efficacy undoubted. From that time onwards the theatre became a kind of family property of the Sheridans and the Linleys, and we get many pictures, in the correspondence of the various members of both families, of the intimate, if not always entirely harmonious, atmosphere which prevailed behind the scenes. Old Mr. Sheridan was the chief storm-centre. His relations with his son throughout their life together were most uncertain. He disapproved of almost everything that Richard did, and of the way in which he did it. The truth was that he much preferred his elder and decidedly less attractive son Charles, who from babyhood had been all that a rather pedantic and pompous parent could desire. He had prophesied dire failure for Dick again and again, and again and again he had been proved wrong—a thing which no heavy father can enjoy.

After Richard's marriage, Thomas Sheridan had forbidden any member of his family to communicate with the prodigal son, and not until the solid success of *The Duenna* had made his attitude seem merely foolish did he offer anything in the shape of an olive branch. Richard, on the other hand, seems to have been genuinely fond of his difficult parent so far as he was allowed to be ; and it is said that when he caught sight of his family in the theatre at a performance of his opera he burst into tears. However, there was no concession to sentimentality in his attitude towards his father once he had taken over Drury Lane. He offered Thomas Sheridan the important position of stage director, but did not allow him to act. This was a fresh cause of fury to the elder man, who was still quite convinced in his own mind that the London public had never been given a real chance to appreciate him. But Richard stuck to his point, and there is little doubt that he was right. There would have been endless trouble over the parts that his father was to play ; and this trouble would have been accentuated by the fact, nowhere precisely stated but often implied, that Richard had no very high opinion of his father's methods. Even on Thomas Sheridan's own pet subject, public oratory, there was a clash of ideas. History does not relate what Thomas thought, many years later, when Richard using methods almost entirely opposite to those which his father had spent half his professional life in demonstrating, was acclaimed the chief orator of his day after his speech in the Warren Hastings trial. It does relate, in considerable detail, that in the early days at Drury Lane Thomas Sheridan thought himself a man with a just grievance.

He seems, indeed, to have been constantly on his dignity, and consequently a thorn in everybody's side. He was stately with the elder Linleys, whom he considered beneath him socially ; and with Mrs. Linley especially he was an object of hearty dislike. The younger Linleys regarded him with a sort of good-natured contempt, reflected in the disrespectful epithets—'Old Crusty', or 'Old Surly Boots'—which they used about him in their letters to one another.

Richard, then, found his father unhelpful, but his wife was very much otherwise. She made herself useful in all kinds of capacities—testing singers, reading plays, and doing secretarial and even accountancy work. As the joint ages of the two of them still totalled roundabout fifty it is a sure guess that they threw themselves into all this with a youthful sense of adventure. Life must have seemed very easy to them in those days.

In 1779 Sheridan added one more to his list of original plays. This was *The Critic*, a burlesque of the contemporary stage and theatre people, of a pattern which had indeed been done before, notably by the Duke of Buckingham in *The Rehearsal*, but which had never been carried to quite this pitch of good-humoured satire. Once again he had added a play to the language which was destined to keep life and freshness down to our own time.

And so, with this third full-length play and in his twenty-eighth year, Sheridan brought to an end that part of his career which has placed him among the immortals, in whose high company he makes so odd an appearance that he himself would have been one of the first to laugh at it. In 1780 he became one of the Members of Parliament for Stafford and embarked upon a new life as a politician. He had never wished to make use of his theatrical gifts. He had employed them as a ladder to wealth when no other was available, and now that his financial stability was secured by his position at Drury Lane he could thankfully kick away the ladder and think no more about it. To be a playwright was to remind people constantly that he was the son of a player, and this was what he wished people to forget. Scorning the base degrees by which he did ascend, he little thought that they were to be his only ladder to lasting fame. He would much have preferred to have been remembered as a statesman ; and it is queer to think how furious he would be if he knew that his place in Westminster Abbey is beside Garrick among the artists and not with Charles James Fox. He did in fact write one more play, *Pizarro*, ten years later, but this was not an original piece of work. It was a translation from Kotzebue and was quite unlike his own work—indeed it is almost unreadable now. But it had the touch of a man who knew his theatre and it hit off the taste of its time. It remained in the theatrical repertory for a surprising number of years, but no part of its author's reputation rests upon it.

The remaining thirty-seven years of Sheridan's life are of comparatively small importance to us ; but they make an interesting story, for somehow Sheridan always contrived to behave more like a character of fiction than of history. In his youth he was the hero of a romantic elopement story ; in middle age he becomes the chief personage in another kind of romance—for most of its length a success story, but of such a kind that the success always seems to carry with it the seeds of ultimate failure. We are not surprised when the tale has an unhappy ending. To Sheridan himself his political career must have seemed always full of high promise. He mixed on terms of complete equality and personal friendship with the great ones of his time. He ranked with them and always had reason to expect that he would be promoted to high office by them. Yet as the years wore on this did not happen. His party leaders made constant use of his great powers of persuasion. When a tactless word from Fox led to the uncovering in public of the carefully guarded secret of the Prince Regent's morganatic marriage to Mrs. Fitzherbert, Sheridan was the man to whom everybody looked to extricate his friends from a dangerous and difficult situation. When the Warren Hastings trial came on it was to Sheridan that the Whigs looked for their most telling oratory, and they did not look in vain. After his two great speeches two things seemed certain—that Hastings would be impeached and that Sheridan would be given a place in the cabinet. Neither happened.

The fact was that while Sheridan had won the friendship and even the affection of his political colleagues he never persuaded them to trust him fully. In part this was a tribute to his integrity, for he was never ready to be a mere ' good party man' and vote just as his leaders told him to. In part it was a misfortune inherent in his lack of background. Not even the resources on which the manager of a great theatre could call were enough to enable him to pay his way in the company which he now kept. From the point of view of his early days he was a very rich man; but from the point of view of his political associates he was little better than a pauper living from hand to mouth. In those circles money was available in such quantities that hardly anybody had to think twice about it. Most of them could lose enormous fortunes with the comfortable assurance that others even more enormous lay behind. Charles James Fox, a young man with aristocratic connexions, ran himself far more deeply into debt than ever Sheridan did and had far less ability or even intention to pay. Yet Sheridan was thought of everywhere as a man of no substance living far beyond his means, while Fox's excesses were regarded with indulgence.

So long as his first wife lived Sheridan had a wise adviser at his elbow cautioning him against insensate extravagance. But the Linleys were a consumptive family and one by one they died early. Elizabeth's death at the age of thirty-eight left her husband at the mercy of his temperament and when he married again he chose a woman, Esther Ogle, as recklessly extravagant as himself. She stood by him gallantly through the last sordid and unhappy scenes of his life, when duns pestered him on his very death-bed; but she never did anything to prevent his decline into this unnecessary misery —unnecessary because his affairs, though hopelessly entangled, were never in fact so desperate as they seemed. Fraser Rae, the first of Sheridan's biographers who brought any quality of detachment to the task, estimates that the debts owing at the time of his death could not have amounted to more than £5,000 in all, and says that they were paid off without difficulty when his estate came to be wound up. The Prince Regent, whose friendship for Sheridan lasted almost to the end of his life, said of him, shrewdly enough, that his chief handicaps in life had been a too great confidence in human nature and a fierce pride which made him 'always willing to grant what he was not willing to accept in return—favours, which might be interpreted as affecting his own independence'. It is no dishonourable epitaph.

Sheridan the man of the world died in 1816, having made a certain mark. Even the least voluminous historian of his times finds it necessary to work in a reference to him somewhere or other, and this is fame of a sort. But Sheridan the dramatist is alive to-day and has never consented to moulder on the shelves along with the other 'classics'. He is more vibrantly alive than any other of the old dramatists excepting only Shakespeare. It is a sound enough test of a play's vitality to see how much space it occupies in the comprehensive list at the end of *Who's Who in the Theatre*, in which are noted all plays that have had any success at all on our stage in London from the earliest recorded times down to the present day. In this list *The School for Scandal* occupies a page and a half. The only plays which have more space than that are *Romeo and Juliet* and *As You Like It*, while *Othello* ties with Sheridan's play for the third place. And it may be noted in passing that Shakespeare had about 150 years start. Neither of Sheridan's other two original plays, *The Rivals* or *The Critic*, has any such triumphant record; but both have been produced again and again. No other dramatist in all the long catalogue of distinguished men who have written for our theatre boasts popularity such as this. It must follow that Shakespeare and Sheridan have something in common, unequal as they are as a pair, which other dramatists fail to show in anything like the same degree.

We need not look long for this common factor for it is clear to be seen. Shakespeare and Sheridan shared in a notable degree one characteristic, that their plays were written only to be acted and not at all to be read. When writing plays they were men of the theatre and of the theatre

alone; any literary merit that their writings happened to
have was incidental. Most significantly, neither man
raised a finger to have his plays published. And so these
two, one the world's transcendental poetic genius and the
other no more than a neat hand at social satire, are linked
together in strange but undeniable fellowship—that fellowship of the theatre to which no literary man, as such, has the
entrée.

The writer who knows the theatre, and more especially
the writer who has had its values about him in his youth,
composes directly for an audience. His chief concern is to
keep taut the thread of narrative by which he works his way
from situation to situation. This 'thread' may be as thick
as a rope or as delicate as a strand of gossamer, but the
dramatist's hands are sensitive to the pull he is exercising
upon it. He knows instinctively when that pull is weaken-
ing and at once hauls in his slack. In other words, he is
first and foremost a story-teller and he knows it. The
literary man is not necessarily a story-teller at all, or even if
he is one he can put story-telling low on the list of his aims.
He is primarily concerned with the art of writing, the ex-
pression of thoughts and ideas in the best possible language,
and he is writing with his mind on a single reader who can
be relied upon to make an effort to understand. Such an
effort is beyond the collective power of an audience; and
the theatrical writer, knowing this, is at pains to make his
meaning very clear.

Congreve may stand as the best example of the literary
man strayed into the theatre. He adopted the dramatic
form because it was the fashion of his day, and not because
he had any special aptitude for it. As a writer he is far
beyond Sheridan's stature. In the blaze of Congreve's wit,
Sheridan's seems a mere flicker. There is hardly a critic
who, judging purely by literary standards, would not put
Congreve's *The Way of the World* above *The School for
Scandal*. Indeed, a great many critics since Congreve's
time have written of *The Way of the World* as a great

comedy. Yet judged by the practical test of the theatre it is no such thing. Audiences have never been persuaded to take to it kindly except once, when an inspired production by Nigel Playfair and an equally inspired performance by Edith Evans as Millamant persuaded 158 audiences to go to see it at the Lyric Theatre, Hammersmith, a very small house which was then strongly in the fashion. A recent revival of the play without these special advantages revealed how much Congreve had owed to them for success at Hammersmith. The plain fact is that the plot of this play is incomprehensible nonsense. So far from the thread of narrative being kept taut, it lies about the stage in festoons and trips up the actors when they try to straighten it out. Congreve was no doubt a great writer, but he was no man of the theatre. Indeed, with his fine-gentleman attitude towards his craft which so irritated Voltaire one feels that he would not have cared to be a man of the theatre, even if he had known how.

Sheridan, as we have seen, was not free from the fine-gentleman attitude, but he was a man of the theatre whether he liked it or not. His story-telling was limpidly clear and his dialogue, while not equal to Congreve's in sheer wit, had the balance and rhythm which is even more effective on the stage. An even greater asset than these was his superb sense of situation. This is exemplified again and again in all three of his plays but it reaches its highest point in the Screen Scene in *The School for Scandal*, probably the most famous single scene in English drama except for the Balcony Scene in *Romeo and Juliet*. It has been said that drama is at its most effective when the audience is in possession of facts which are unknown to the characters on the stage; and if this is true, the Screen Scene, from the point where Lady Teazle hides until the moment when Sir Peter and Charles Surface, in carefree search of the 'little French milliner', find her, is a perfect example of dramatic tension and surprise. Another instance, much slighter in its effect but even more startling in its ingenuity, is the scene in *The Critic* where Whiskerandos is attacked by the two Uncles and the two Nieces. The stage direction is as follows :

> The two Nieces draw their two daggers to strike Whiskerandos, the two Uncles at the instant with their two swords drawn catch their two Nieces' arms and turn the points of their swords to Whiskerandos, who immediately draws two daggers and holds them to the two Nieces' bosoms.

This is a piece of pure theatre—doubly so, because we here see the theatre burlesquing its own tendency to over-emphasize a situation, and doing so in its own particular terms. Literature has nothing to say to it. The appeal is directly to the eye. The effect aimed at is laughter through the purely visual surprise which the spectator feels when the five players swiftly arrange themselves into the absurd group described in the stage direction. The effect having been obtained, Sheridan then feels himself free to extract more fun from it by means of the spoken word, when the complacent Mr. Puff explains to his friend Sneer the beauty of his contrivance :

> There's a situation for you ! There's an heroic group !—you see the ladies can't stab Whiskerandos—he durst not strike them for fear of their Uncles—the Uncles durst not kill him because of their nieces—I have them all at a dead lock !—for everyone of them is afraid to let go first.

Sneer very rightly remarks that in that case they must stand there for ever, but Puff is ready for this too. He brings on a Beefeater :

> *Beefeater :* In the Queen's name I charge you all to drop Your swords and daggers.

Crash go the swords and daggers on the stage ; and a tiny incident, which would never have occurred to the mind of anybody who was not writing directly for an audience, ends to the sound of inevitable laughter.

Another cogent reason why Sheridan's plays should have held the stage continuously, while those of more deeply gifted men have suffered total or at best periodic eclipse, is their essential decency. It was his good fortune to live at a period of theatrical history exactly midway between the licentiousness of the Restoration stage and the overdone prudery of the Victorian era. In Sheridan's time it was no longer the fashion to be foul-mouthed but no objection was taken to ordinary free speech. As a result the best plays of this time—Oliver Goldsmith's *She Stoops to Conquer* (1773) may serve as another striking example—have about them a natural lack of offence combined with an uninhibited gaiety. This combination of qualities has given them a certain universality of appeal to all later generations.

Reasons like these may well serve to explain why producers in search of attractive revivals are always ready to take down Sheridan's works once again from the shelf on which they have never yet been allowed to gather much dust; but they cannot tell the whole story. Plays do not continue to live through changes of fashion and revolutions in thought such as we have seen in the last century and a half merely because they tell a story well, or because they are neatly carpentered for the stage, or because they reflect youthful high spirits, or because they are fit for family consumption. Some other preservative element is needed and this can only be the author's knowledge of human nature. Nobody can suggest that Sheridan's knowledge went very deep but so far as it did go it was genuine. His characters are very seldom portraits; as a rule they are gently caricatured. But the stage has a way of being most lifelike when it is a little larger than life, and nearly all Sheridan's people are recognizable types containing their own inner vitality. The reason is that they were all observed directly from life, the sole important exception being Mrs. Malaprop, whom Sheridan borrowed, with improvements, from his mother's writings. Because they are not portraits, and because their creator was no more than a lively youth at the time when he brought them into existence, none of these people has very much heart. But it would be unsuitable if they had, for Sheridan's first impulse towards dramatic writing was always satiric; and in such works any attempt at emotional writing must have devolved into sentimentality.

Sentimentality was indeed one of Sheridan's chief weaknesses in private life. His emotions were always sincere and indeed overwhelming at the moment when he felt them, but they were apt to be moods. His love for Elizabeth Linley seems to have been at once the deepest and most lasting of his emotions. Some of her delightful letters to him at a time when they had been married for fifteen years or more show how happy they were together in spite of his volatile temperament and the temptations to which his successes, and the life of leisure which he was living in houses of the great, exposed him. Later on, he failed her. He fell passionately in love with Lady Duncannon, later the Countess of Bessborough, the sister of Georgiana of Devonshire. A public scandal was only just averted, and a letter written by Elizabeth to her great friend Mrs. Stratford Canning is in a tone of bitter disgust with Sheridan. Another letter to the same friend a little later shows that the affair was hushed up. Husband and wife were reconciled and throughout Elizabeth's last illness, which came in the following year (1792), his devotion to her was untiring. Yet he was still being torn in two directions, for his own account of Elizabeth's illness and death still exists in the form of a series of letters written to Lady Duncannon in Italy where she had been sent to join her sister while the scandal died down. These letters are in a tone which show that Sheridan's passion for Lady Duncannon had by no means cooled.

For all the storms of grief and remorse that swept over him after Elizabeth's death, it may be doubted whether Sheridan ever knew quite fully the greatness of his loss. She had been at his side at all the highest and most spectacular triumphs of his life, and now that she was no longer there no more such triumphs were to come his way. Instead, a subtle process of disintegration began.

It was slow as well as subtle, for it extended over twenty-four years, during most of which Sheridan must still have had at least the illusion of success and the hope of political reward. Youth had departed, and he had developed a bloated and blotched complexion which destroyed any claim to good looks which he may once have had ; but on the other hand he was over forty, which in those days was advanced middle-age, and he still maintained his personal charm, his vitality, and reasonable health. He was still in the public eye, a figure important enough to be material for the cartoonists. The Prince Regent delighted in his company and relied on his advice. The Whig leaders treated him with respect and sought his help. Society laughed at his sallies, and regarded his vagaries with indulgent amusement. And the great pile of Drury Lane gave assurance of financial security, and was, from day to day, a regular if reluctant source of ready cash. All must have seemed well to the man to whom Elizabeth, in one of her charming letters, had once remarked, ' You are such a sanguine pig '.

That all was not well is clear enough in retrospect, for gradually all his resources failed him. Drury Lane itself changed for a time from an asset to a major liability. It became obvious in 1791 that the theatre would have to be rebuilt, and arrangements were made without undue difficulty to finance the operation. But when the bills came in, they exceeded the estimates by £70,000. By one of those clever manipulations of figures which make one think that Sheridan might have made a good Chancellor of the Exchequer, he surmounted this obstacle and the new theatre opened in 1794. But he could not surmount another obstacle which confronted him fifteen years later when the building was burnt to the ground. Another theatre did indeed rise from its ashes but it was financed by the brewer, Samuel Whitbread, who paid Sheridan reasonably well for his patent but would allow him no active share in the management.

Sheridan's grand friends in the political oligarchy continued to flatter him and to use him but secretly were still well aware that he had not been born to wealth and privilege. Indeed, among themselves they sometimes wrote of him in a curiously patronizing tone. Even the Duchess of Devonshire showed that she had never been able entirely to forget that he was a player's son. As for the caricaturists, they treated him with a deepening contempt, treating his red nose and blotched cheeks as evidence of a love of the bottle outstanding even in those days of hard drinkers. Probably they maligned him in this. He did not, at any rate, drink his constitution to pieces, for he lived to be sixty-five—which was, in those days, a ripe old age.

The Prince Regent stood by Sheridan almost to the end; but he withdrew his favour in 1811 and after that the Whig leaders made it clear that it had only been for his influence with the Prince that they had kept him amongst them. As for Society, its laughter grew less and less kind as Sheridan's eccentricities grew wilder; and the pity of it was that the ill-natured stories about him which went the rounds were now more often true than not. After allowing him to die in misery, London remembered that he had been one of her favourites and gave him a splendid funeral. It was the last ironic comment on the gallant, if misconceived, adventure which was Sheridan's life.

SHERIDAN
A
Select Bibliography

(Place of publication London, unless stated otherwise.)

Bibliography :

SEVEN XVIIIth CENTURY BIBLIOGRAPHIES, by I. A. Williams (1924).
The Sheridan bibliography is a standard work of reference for first editions.

THE PLAYS AND POEMS, edited by R. C. Rhodes, 3 vols. Oxford (1928).
Bibliographies of separate works are included.

Collected Editions : A selection.

THE DRAMATIC WORKS, together with a Life of the Author (1798).
The first edition, of the previous year, does not contain the ' Life '.

THE WORKS, with a Preface by Thomas Moore, 2 vols. (1821).
The first authorized collection.

THE DRAMATIC WORKS, with a Biographical and Critical Sketch by Leigh Hunt (1840) ; reprinted 1846, 1865.

SPEECHES, 5 vols. (1816).
Reprinted in 3 vols., 1842.

THE DRAMATIC WORKS, edited by G. C. S[igmond] (1848), reprinted 1889, 1902.

THE PLAYS, edited by A. W. Pollard (1900).
Subsequently reprinted, and still a dependable edition.

THE PLAYS, prepared partly from MS. drafts, edited by W. F. Rae (1902).
With an Introduction by the Marquess of Dufferin and Ava, Sheridan's great-grandson.

THE PLAYS, edited by I. Knight. Oxford (1906).

THE PLAYS AND POEMS, edited by R. C. Rhodes, 3 vols. Oxford (1928).
The definitive edition, with Introductions and Appendices.

Note : The principal dramatic works have been included in many popular series, e.g., the Worlds Classics (1901) and Everymans Library (1906).

Principal Separate Works:

THE RIVALS, Dublin (1775). *Drama.*
The most accurate version of this comedy is the parallel text edition (Oxford 1935) prepared by R. L. Purdy from collations of the Larpent MS. and the earliest published versions.

THE DUENNA (1775). *Comic Opera.*

THE SCHOOL FOR SCANDAL, Dublin (1780). *Drama.*
The first of several textually corrupt editions, the first genuine text being published in Dublin in 1799; Sheridan's final revision was first printed in the Collected Edition of 1821.

THE CRITIC (1781). *Drama.*
A burlesque.

A TRIP TO SCARBOROUGH (1781). *Drama.*
An adaptation of Vanbrugh's *The Relapse*, 1697.

SPEECH ... AGAINST WARREN HASTINGS (1787). *Oratory.*
A report of Sheridan's most celebrated Speech in the House of Commons.

ST. PATRICK'S DAY; OR THE SCHEMING LIEUTENANT, Dublin (1788). *Drama.*
A farce.

Note: Sheridan also collaborated in a number of theatrical entertainments, e.g., 'The Forty Thieves' (1808), and contributed several prologues and epilogues to plays by other writers. His most important piece of occasional verse is 'Verses to the Memory of Garrick, spoken as a Monody' (1779).

Some Critical and Biographical Studies:

MEMOIRS OF THE PUBLIC AND PRIVATE LIFE OF SHERIDAN, by J. Watkins. 2 vols. (1817).

MEMOIRS OF THE LIFE OF SHERIDAN, by T. Moore, 2 vols. (1825).
Reprinted 1827 (5th ed.) with new preface.

SHERIDAN, by M. Oliphant (1883).
In 'The English Men of Letters' Series.

LIVES OF THE SHERIDANS, by P. Fitzgerald, 2 vols. (1886).
An account of Sheridan and his family, including many letters.

LIFE OF SHERIDAN, by L. C. Sanders (1890).

SELECT BIBLIOGRAPHY

SHERIDAN : A Biography by W. F. Rae. 2 vols. (1896).
Documented, and with an Introduction by the Marquess of Dufferin and Ava.

SHERIDAN, by W. Sichel, 2 vols. (1909).
Valuable for its examination of Sheridan as a politician; includes letters, diaries, and other appendices. Full and authoritative.

THE POLITICAL CAREER OF SHERIDAN, by M. T. H. Sadler [Michael Sadleir]. Oxford (1912).

SHERIDAN. A Ghost Story by E. M. Butler (1931).
Contains some discerning conjectures about Sheridan's later years.

SHERIDAN, by W. A. Darlington (1933).
A dramatic critic's estimate, in Duckworth's 'Brief Lives' Series.

HARLEQUIN SHERIDAN : the Man and the Legends, by R. C. Rhodes. Oxford (1933).
A valuable study, by Sheridan's principal modern editor.

SHERIDAN, by L. Gibbs (1947).

¶ The Supplements to *British Book News*, which are usually published on the last Monday in each month, may be subscribed for through booksellers on a yearly or half-yearly basis. A year's issues cost 18s. post free; six months' cost 9s. post free. Prospectuses are available; and particulars of Supplements published or available shortly will be found overleaf. Inquiries should be addressed to booksellers, or in case of difficulty direct to the Publishers, LONGMANS, GREEN & CO., 6 & 7 Clifford Street, London, W.1.

BRITISH BOOK NEWS

A monthly bibliographical journal designed to acquaint the reader with the best British books on all subjects, including those published in the Commonwealth and Empire. It contains bibliographies of specific subjects, and articles of general interest to the bookman. Its most important feature is the Book List, compiled by a number of specialists, which occupies the major part of each issue and provides a critical selection of the most important new books and reprints of all kinds, annotated, classified, and indexed.

2s. per copy (United Kingdom)

1s. per copy (Overseas)

Annual subscription 10s. (Overseas)

Bound volumes, fully indexed, are available as follows through LONGMANS, GREEN & CO., 6 & 7 Clifford Street, London, W.1 : for 1943 and 1944, 6s. net each; for 1945, 7s. 6d. net; for 1946, 12s. 6d. net; for 1947, 15s. net; for 1948, 15s. net.

¶ *British Book News* is published for the British Council by the National Book League. Address, BRITISH BOOK NEWS, 3 Hanover Street, London, W.1.

Supplements to
BRITISH BOOK NEWS

★

BERNARD SHAW	A. C. Ward
JOSEPH CONRAD	Oliver Warner
G. K. CHESTERTON	Christopher Hollis
THE BRONTË SISTERS	Phyllis Bentley
HENRY JAMES	Michael Swan
JOHN KEATS	Edmund Blunden
E. M. FORSTER	Rex Warner
T. S. ELIOT	M. C. Bradbrook
ARNOLD BENNETT	Frank Swinnerton
BYRON	Herbert Read
WILLIAM BLAKE	Kathleen Raine
BERTRAND RUSSELL	Alan Dorward
TOBIAS SMOLLETT	Laurence Brander
GEORGE ELIOT	Lettice Cooper
OSBERT SITWELL	Roger Fulford
JANE AUSTEN	Sylvia Townsend Warner
G. M. TREVELYAN	J. H. Plumb
KIPLING	Bonamy Dobrée
I. COMPTON-BURNETT	Pamela Hansford Johnson
THOMAS HARDY	R. A. Scott-James

Each with a frontispiece; an introductory essay;
and a select bibliography

PUBLISHED FOR
THE BRITISH COUNCIL
and the NATIONAL BOOK LEAGUE
by LONGMANS, GREEN & CO.
LONDON. NEW YORK. TORONTO.

Revised Price
2s. 6d. net